Birthday Book

ISBN-13: 978-1985692879
ISBN-10: 1985692872

INTRODUCTION

It's obvious really, but this is how to use this book to record birthdays, anniversaries and any other notable dates that you need to remember. Here are a few examples:

January

1	A Friend (1974)	Birthday
2		
3	Our kitten joined the family (2007)	
4	My wedding anniversary (2003)	
5		
6	Moved into our house (2006)	

> Remember to note the year of your friends birthday then you will be able to remember how old they are!

> It is useful to note other dates that are important to you, not just birthdays and anniversaries

January

1.

2.

3.

4.

5.

6.

7.

8.

January

9

10

11

12

13

14

15

16

January

17

18

19

20

21

22

23

24

January

25

26

27

28

29

30

31

February

1.

2.

3.

4.

5.

6.

7.

8.

February

9

10

11

12

13

14

15

16

February

17

18

19

20

21

22

23

24

February

25

26

27

28

29

March

1

2

3

4

5

6

7

8

March

9	
10	
11	
12	
13	
14	
15	
16	

March

17

18

19

20

21

22

23

24

March

25

26

27

28

29

30

31

April

1.

2.

3.

4.

5.

6.

7.

8.

April

9

10

11

12

13

14

15

16

April

17

18

19

20

21

22

23

24

April

25

26

27

28

29

30

May

1.

2.

3.

4.

5.

6.

7.

8.

May

9

10

11

12

13

14

15

16

May

17

18

19

20

21

22

23

24

May

25

26

27

28

29

30

31

June

1.

2.

3.

4.

5.

6.

7.

8.

June

9

10

11

12

13

14

15

16

June

17

18

19

20

21

22

23

24

June

25	
26	
27	
28	
29	
30	

July

1.

2.

3.

4.

5.

6.

7.

8.

July

9

10

11

12

13

14

15

16

July

17	
18	
19	
20	
21	
22	
23	
24	

July

25	
26	
27	
28	
29	
30	
31	

August

1

2

3

4

5

6

7

8

August

9

10

11

12

13

14

15

16

August

17

18

19

20

21

22

23

24

August

25

26

27

28

29

30

31

September

1.
2.
3.
4.
5.
6.
7.
8.

September

9

10

11

12

13

14

15

16

September

17

18

19

20

21

22

23

24

September

25

26

27

28

29

30

October

1.

2.

3.

4.

5.

6.

7.

8.

October

- 9
- 10
- 11
- 12
- 13
- 14
- 15
- 16

October

17

18

19

20

21

22

23

24

October

25

26

27

28

29

30

31

November

1

2

3

4

5

6

7

8

November

9

10

11

12

13

14

15

16

November

17

18

19

20

21

22

23

24

November

25	
26	
27	
28	
29	
30	

December

1.

2.

3.

4.

5.

6.

7.

8.

December

9

10

11

12

13

14

15

16

December

17

18

19

20

21

22

23

24

December

25

26

27

28

29

30

31

NOTES

NOTES

NOTES

NOTES

NOTES

Printed in Poland
by Amazon Fulfillment
Poland Sp. z o.o., Wrocław